TIMELESS POPULAR CLASSICS

40 Piano Arrangements of the Most-Requested Favorites

ARRANGED BY DAN COATES

This collection offers accessible piano arrangements of timeless, popular songs. It contains 40 favorites that are instantly familiar and motivating to learn. Pianists will enjoy the jazzy harmonies of "As Time Goes By," the powerful climax of "Bridge over Troubled Water," the driving rhythms of "Don't Stop Believin'," the iconic hook of "Colors of the Wind," and the triumphant fanfare of the *Star Wars* theme—page after page of great music!

Arranged by prolific popular-music arranger Dan Coates, each piece is not only fun to play but also

quality teaching material that can help improve sight-reading ability while reinforcing essential piano-playing skills. Students can develop pedaling skills while learning "In Dreams" (from *The Lord of the Rings*) or master syncopations by practicing "Killing Me Softly." "My Funny Valentine" provides an opportunity to learn a piece with multiple voices in one hand, and "Un-break My Heart," which uses the keys of B minor and D minor, can be used to explore the concept of modulation. Each arrangement is edited with helpful fingering and pedaling indications to aid learning. Enjoy these *Timeless Popular Classics*!

Contents

GERSHWIN® and GEORGE GERSHWIN® are registered trademarks of Gershwin Enterprises.
IRA GERSHWIN™ is a trademark of Gershwin Enterprises.

Produced by
Alfred Music
P.O. Box 10003
Van Nuys, CA 91410-0003
alfred.com

Printed in USA.

ISBN-10: 1-4706-3504-6
ISBN-13: 978-1-4706-3504-6
Cover Photo
Piano: © Getty Images / peterhung101

As Time Goes By

(from *Casablanca*)

Words and Music by Herman Hupfeld
Arr. Dan Coates

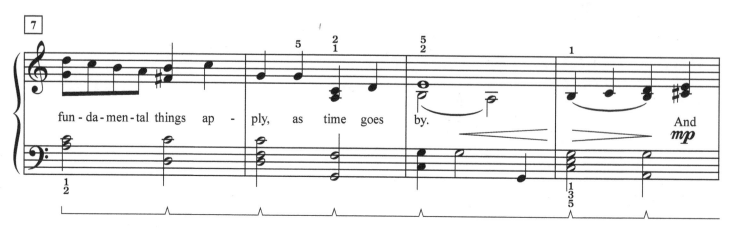

when two lov - ers woo, they still say, "I love you," on that you can re - ly;

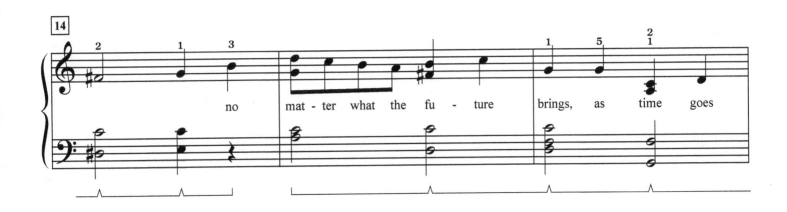

no mat - ter what the fu - ture brings, as time goes

by. Moon - light and love songs

mf

nev - er out of date, hearts full of pas - sion, jeal - ou - sy and hate;

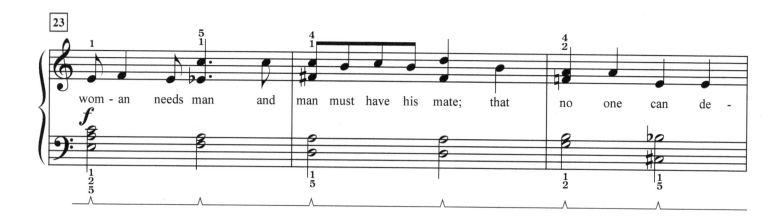

wom - an needs man and man must have his mate; that no one can de -

ny. It's still the same old sto - ry, a fight for love and glo - ry, a

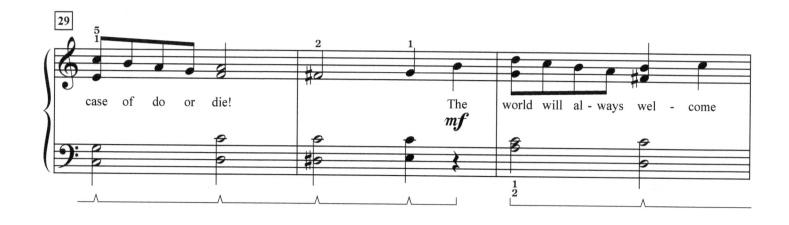

case of do or die! The world will al - ways wel - come

lov - ers, as time goes by.

At Last

Music by Harry Warren
Lyrics by Mack Gordon
Arr. Dan Coates

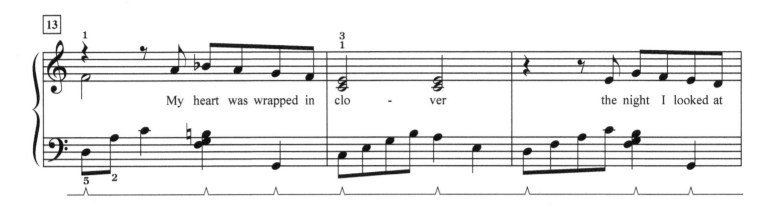

My heart was wrapped in clo - ver the night I looked at

you. I found a dream that I can

speak to, a dream that I can call my own. I found a

thrill to press my cheek to, a thrill I've nev - er

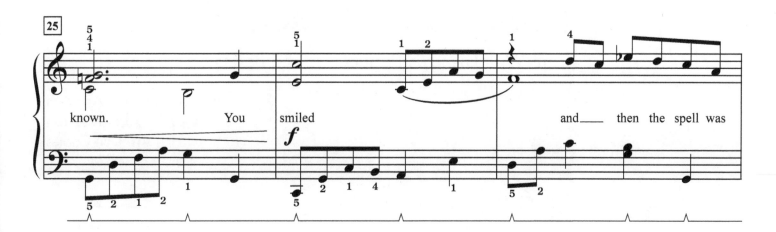

known. You smiled   and___ then the spell was

cast.   And___ here we are in heav - en

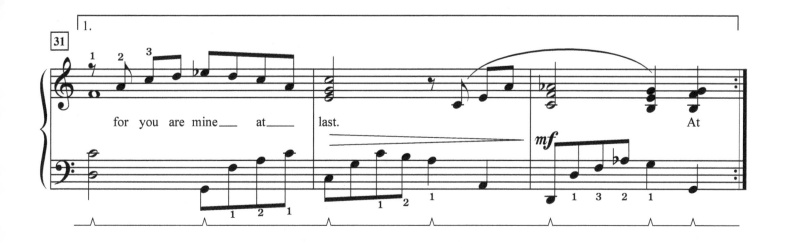

1.

for you are mine___ at___ last.   At

2.

for you are mine___ at___ last.

Beauty and the Beast

(from Walt Disney's *Beauty and the Beast*)

Lyrics by Howard Ashman
Music by Alan Menken
Arr. Dan Coates

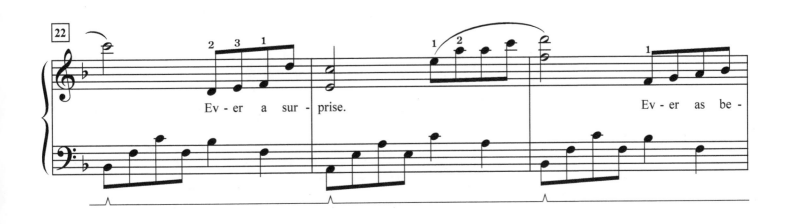

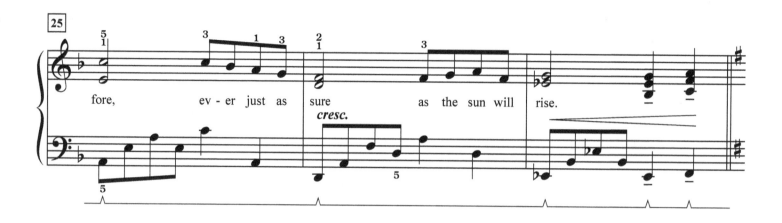

fore,   ev - er just as sure   as the sun will rise.

cresc.

Tale as old as time.   Tune as old as

f

song.   Bit - ter - sweet and strange,   find - ing you can

change,   learn - ing you were wrong.   Cer - tain as the

mf

sun rising in the East. Tale as old as

time, song as old as rhyme. Beauty and the Beast.

dim.

Tale as old as time, song as old as rhyme. Beauty and the Beast.

mp *meno mosso* *rit.*

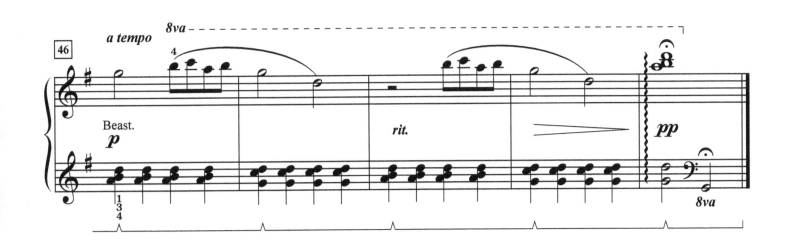

a tempo

Beast.

p *rit.* *pp*

Blue Moon

Music by Richard Rodgers
Lyrics by Lorenz Hart
Arr. Dan Coates

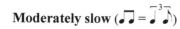

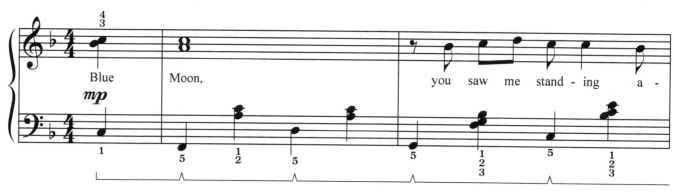

Moon, you knew just what I was there for.

You heard me say - ing a prayer for_____ some - one I real - ly could

care for. And then there sud - den - ly ap - peared be -

fore me the on - ly one my arms will ev - er hold. I heard some -

simile

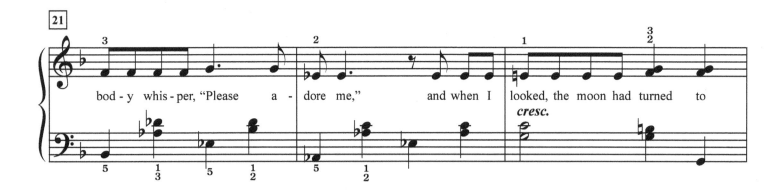

bod - y whis - per, "Please a - dore me," and when I looked, the moon had turned to

cresc.

gold! Blue Moon, now I'm no long - er a -

mf

simile

lone with - out a dream in my heart,

with - out a love of my own.

mp

p

But Not for Me

Music and Lyrics by
George Gershwin and Ira Gershwin
Arr. Dan Coates

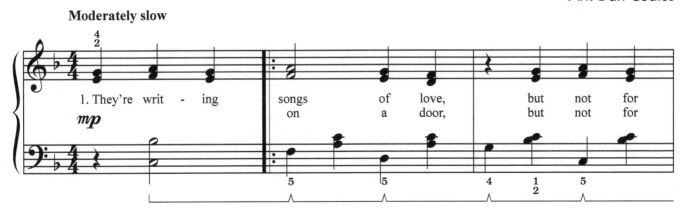

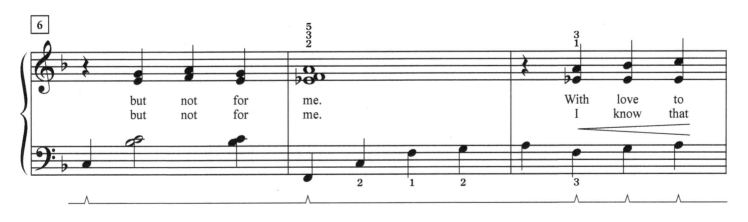

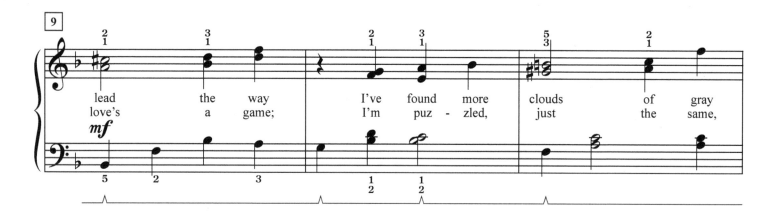

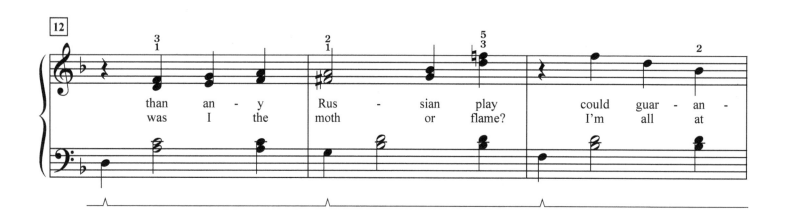

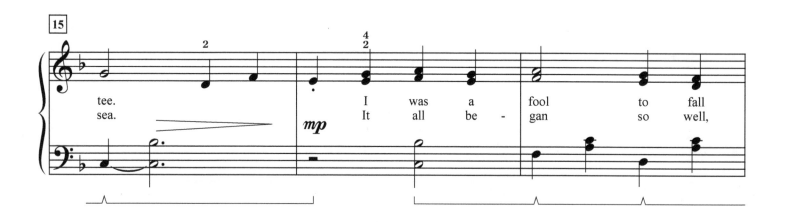

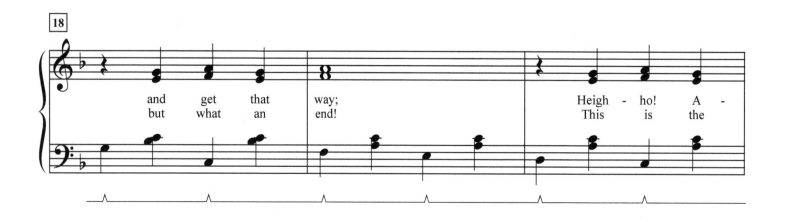

Bridge over Troubled Water

Words and Music by Paul Simon
Arr. Dan Coates

side, oh, when times___ get rough,_____

___ and friends just can't be found. Like a

cresc.

Chorus:

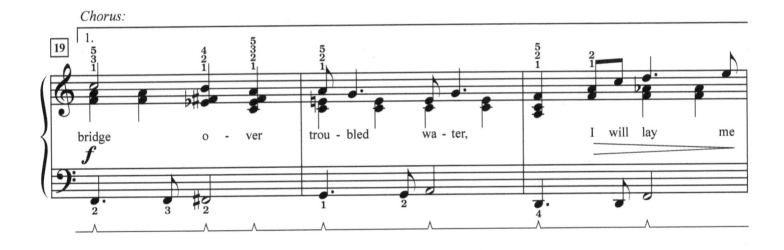

bridge o - ver trou - bled wa - ter, I will lay me

f

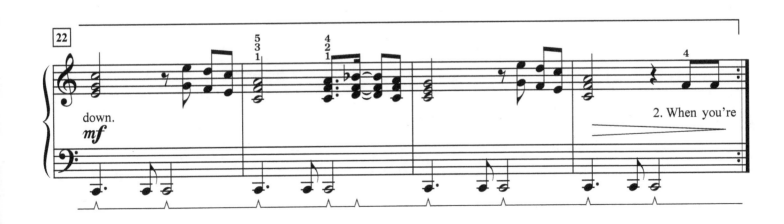

down.

mf

2. When you're

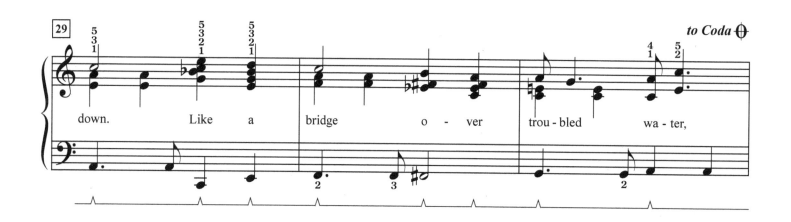

Coda

I will ease your mind.

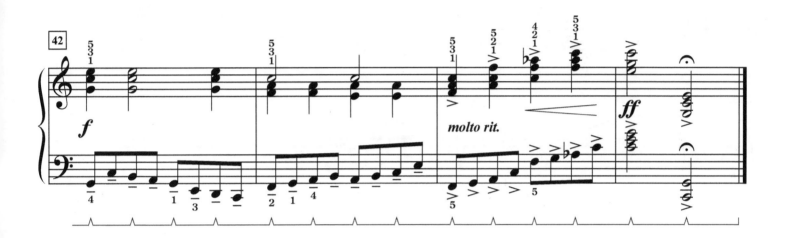

molto rit.

Verse 2:
When you're down and out,
When you're on the street,
When evening falls so hard, I will comfort you.
I'll take your part when darkness comes
And pain is all around.
Like a bridge over troubled water, I will lay me down.
Like a bridge over troubled water, I will lay me down.

Verse 3:
Sail on, silver girl, sail on by.
Your time has come to shine,
All your dreams are on their way.
See how they shine, if you need a friend.
I'm sailing right behind.
Like a bridge over troubled water, I will ease your mind.
Like a bridge over troubled water, I will ease your mind.

Colors of the Wind

(from Walt Disney's *Pocahontas*)

Lyrics by Stephen Schwartz
Music by Alan Menken
Arr. Dan Coates

Can You Feel the Love Tonight

(from Walt Disney's *The Lion King*)

Music by Elton John
Words by Tim Rice
Arr. Dan Coates

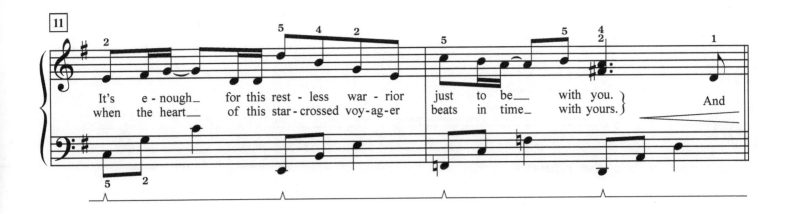

It's e - nough__ for this rest - less war - rior just to be__ with you.
when the heart__ of this star - crossed voy - ag - er beats in time__ with yours.

And

Chorus:

can you feel__ the love__ to - night?__ It is where we are.__

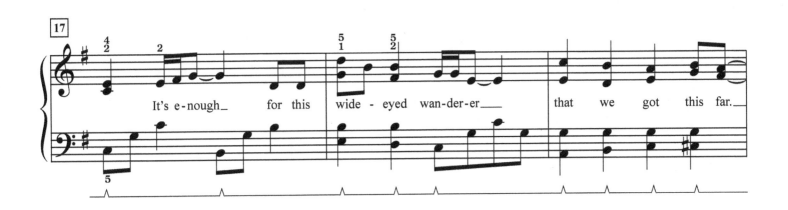

It's e - nough__ for this wide - eyed wan - der - er__ that we got this far.

And can you feel__ the love__ to - night,__

how it's laid to rest? _____ It's e-nough_ to make

kings_ and vag-a-bonds_ be - lieve the ver - y best.

1.

mp

2.

mp

It's e-nough_ to make kings_ and vag-a-bonds_ be- lieve the ver - y best.

rit. *p*

Don't Stop Believin'

Words and Music by
Jonathan Cain, Neal Schon and Steve Perry
Arr. Dan Coates

D.S. al Coda

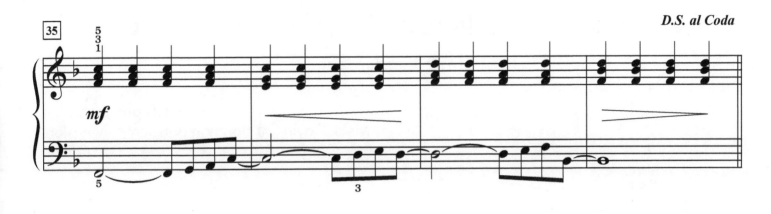

Coda

Chorus:

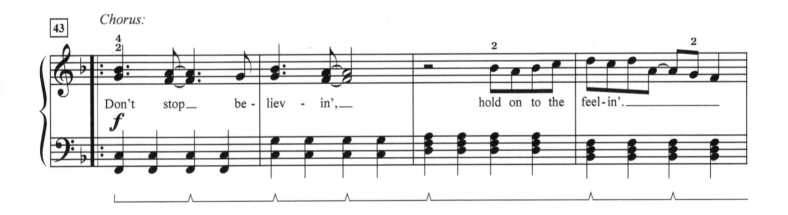

Don't stop_ be - liev - in',_ hold on to the feel-in'._

Street - light_ peo - ple._

Verse 3:
A singer in a smoky room,
The smell of wine and cheap perfume.
For a smile they can share the night
It goes on and on and on and on.

Verse 4:
Working hard to get my fill.
Everybody wants a thrill,
Payin' anything to roll the dice
Just one more time.

Verse 5:
Some will win and some will lose,
Some were born to sing the blues.
Oh, the movie never ends,
It goes on and on and on and on.

A Dream Is a Wish Your Heart Makes

(from *Cinderella*)

Words and Music by
Mack David, Al Hoffman and Jerry Livingston
Arr. Dan Coates

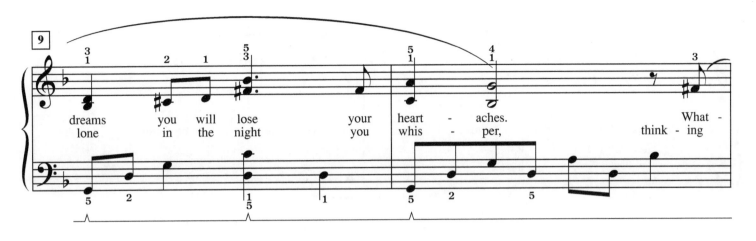

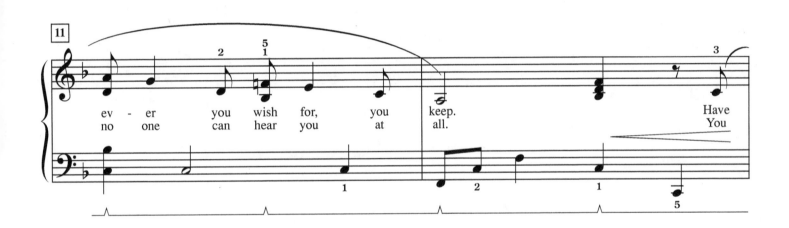

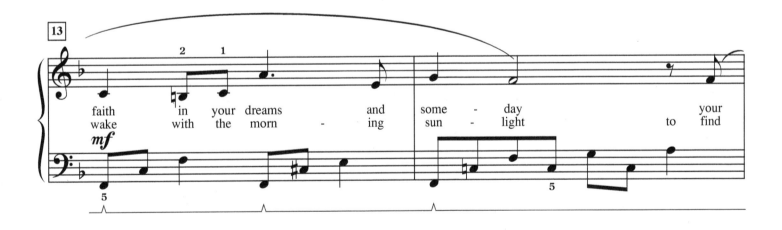

34

how your heart is griev - ing, if you keep on be - liev - ing, the
heart be filled with sor - row, if for all you know, to - mor - row the

dream that you wish will come true.
dream that you wish will will come *mp*

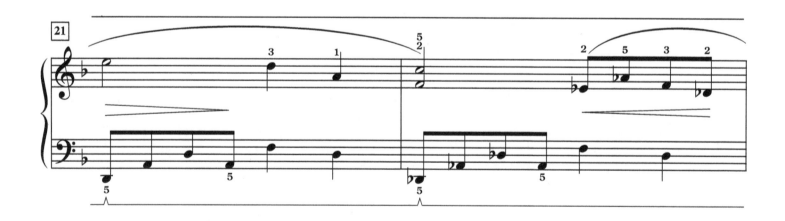

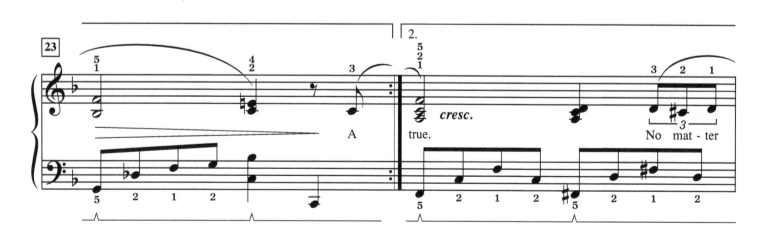

A true. *cresc.* No mat - ter

how your heart is griev - ing, if you keep on be - liev - ing, the

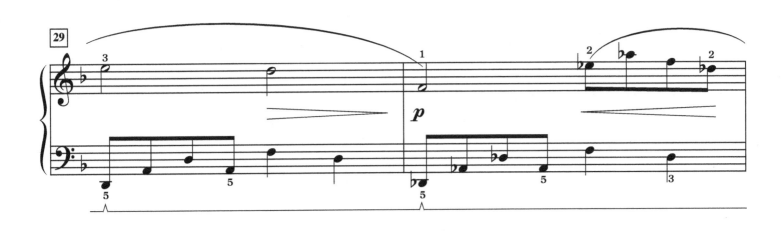

dream that you wish will come true.

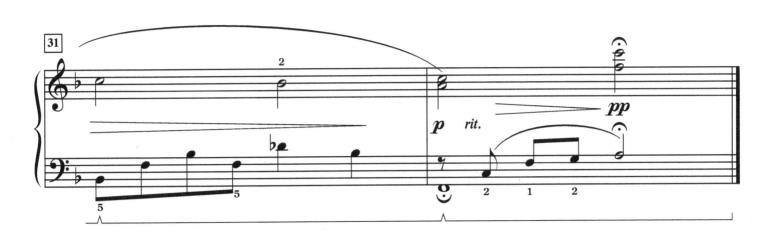

Embraceable You

Music and Lyrics by
George Gershwin and Ira Gershwin
Arr. Dan Coates

Moderately slow, with expression

Em - brace me, my sweet em - brace - a - ble you!

Em - brace me, you ir - re - place - a - ble you!

Just one look at you, my heart grew tip - sy in me.

You and you a - lone bring out the gyp - sy in me!

The Greatest Love of All

Words by Linda Creed
Music by Michael Masser
Arr. Dan Coates

Slowly, with expression

Verse:

I be-lieve the child-ren are the fu - ture; teach them well and let them lead the way.

Show them all the beau-ty they pos-sess in - side. Give them a

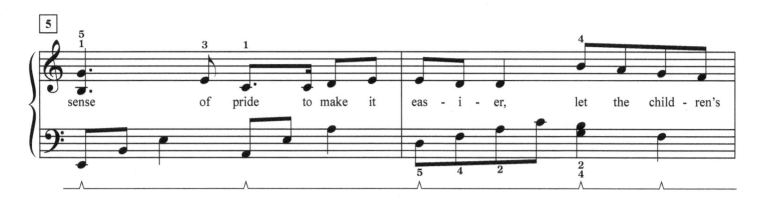

sense of pride to make it eas - i - er, let the child - ren's

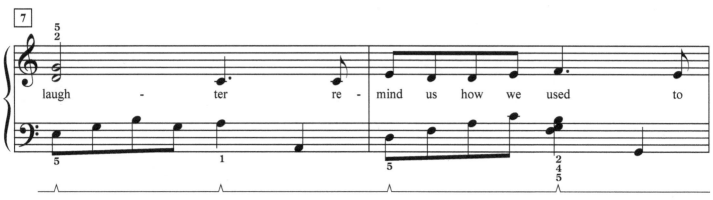

laugh - ter re - mind us how we used to

Learn - ing to love your - self is the great - est love of

dim.

1. (Da Capo)

all.

2.

all. And if by chance that spe - cial place that you've been dream - ing

of leads you to a lone - ly place,

find your strength in love.

rit.

p

How Do I Live

Words and Music by Diane Warren
Arr. Dan Coates

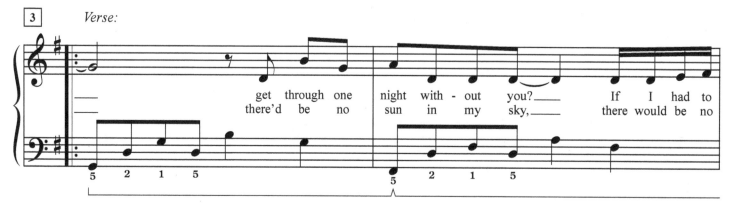

I Could Have Danced All Night

(from *My Fair Lady*)

Lyrics by Alan Jay Lerner
Music by Frederick Loewe
Arr. Dan Coates

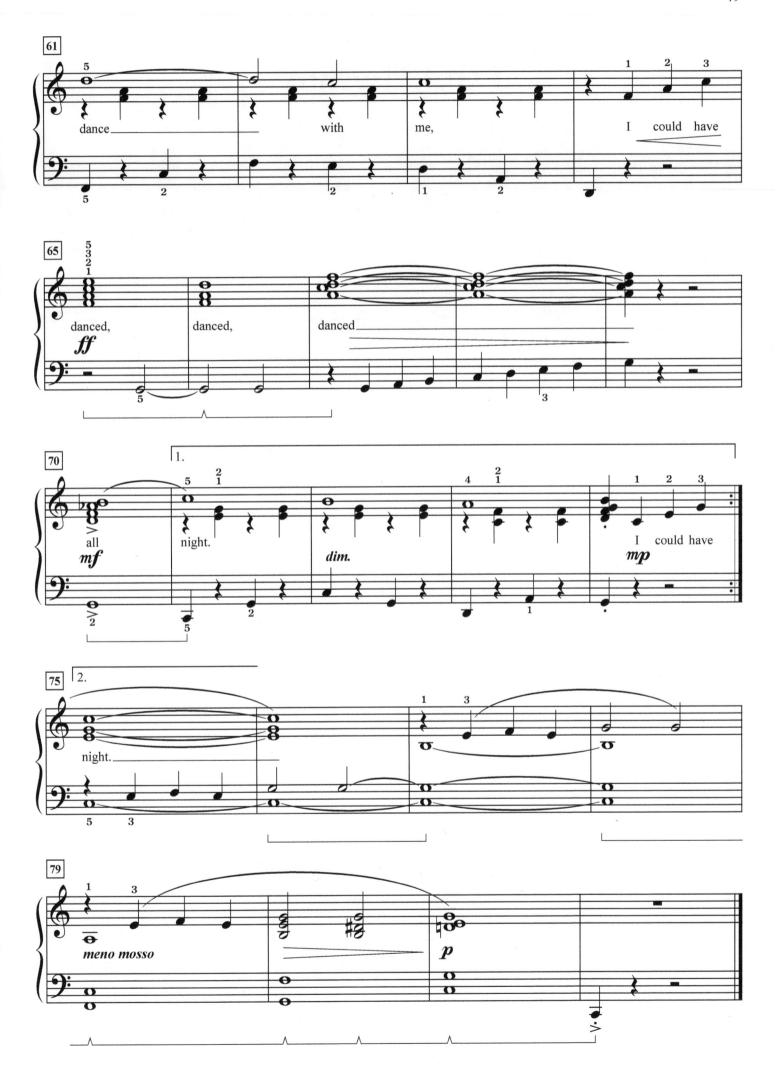

I Got Rhythm

Music and Lyrics by
George Gershwin and Ira Gershwin
Arr. Dan Coates

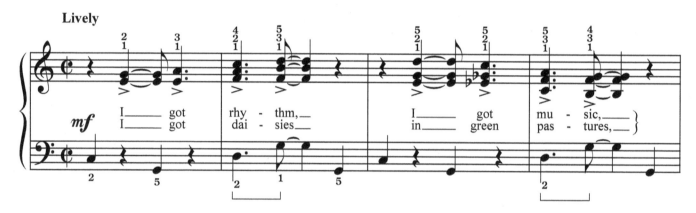

51

If Ever I Would Leave You

(from *Camelot*)

Music by Frederick Loewe
Lyrics by Alan Jay Lerner
Arr. Dan Coates

If I Only Had a Brain

(from *The Wizard of Oz*)

Music by Harold Arlen
Lyrics by E.Y. Harburg
Arr. Dan Coates

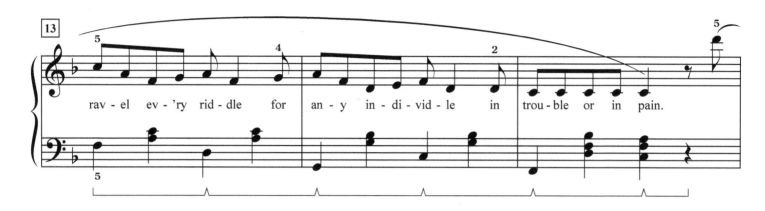

rav - el ev - 'ry rid - dle for an - y in - di - vid - le in trou - ble or in pain.

With the thoughts I'd be think - in' I could be an - oth - er Lin - coln, if I

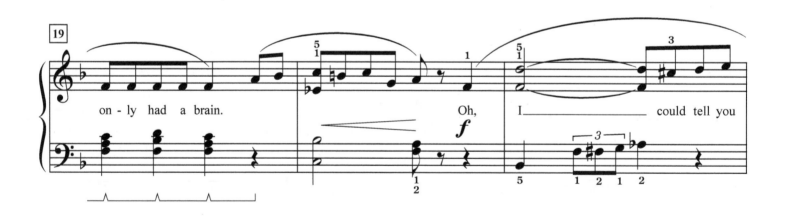

on - ly had a brain. Oh, I could tell you

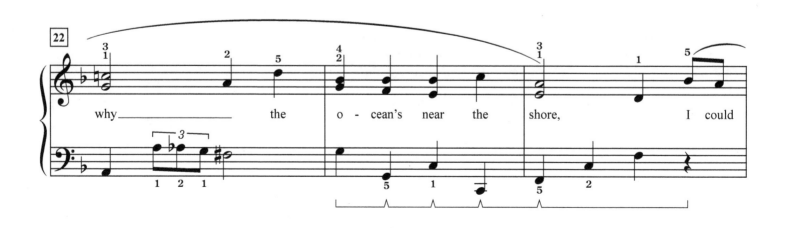

why the o - cean's near the shore, I could

think of things I nev - er thunk be - fore   and then I'd sit   and think some

more.   I would not be just a nuff-in', my   head all full of stuff-in', my

heart all full of pain   and per - haps I'd de - serve you and be

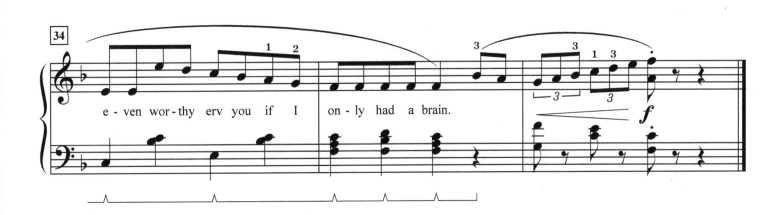

e - ven wor-thy erv you if I   on - ly had a brain.

The Imperial March (Darth Vader's Theme)

(from *Star Wars: The Empire Strikes Back*)

Music by **JOHN WILLIAMS**
Arr. Dan Coates

Killing Me Softly

Words and Music by
Charles Fox and Norman Gimbel
Arr. Dan Coates

In Dreams

(from *The Lord of the Rings: The Fellowship of the Ring*)

Words and Music by
Fran Walsh and Howard Shore
Arr. Dan Coates

sun　　　we will　walk_____ in bit - ter　rain.　　　　But in dreams,_____

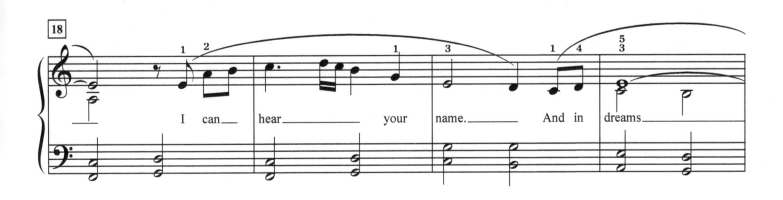

I　can_____ hear_____ your　name._____　And in　dreams_____

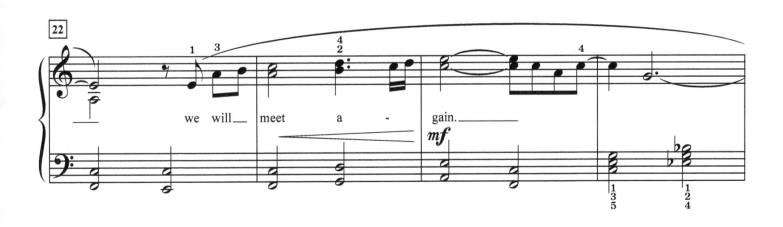

we will____ meet　a -　　gain._____

mf

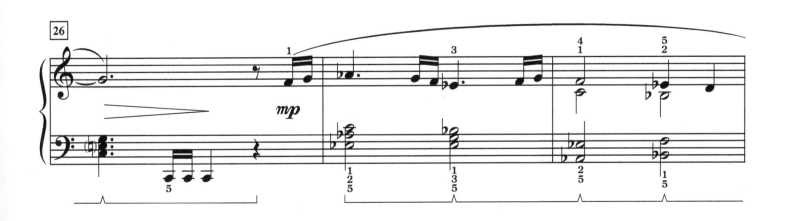

mp

Let It Go

(from Walt Disney's *Frozen*)

Music and Lyrics by
Kristen Anderson-Lopez and Robert Lopez
Arr. Dan Coates

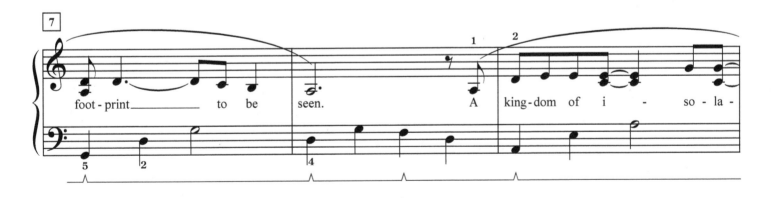

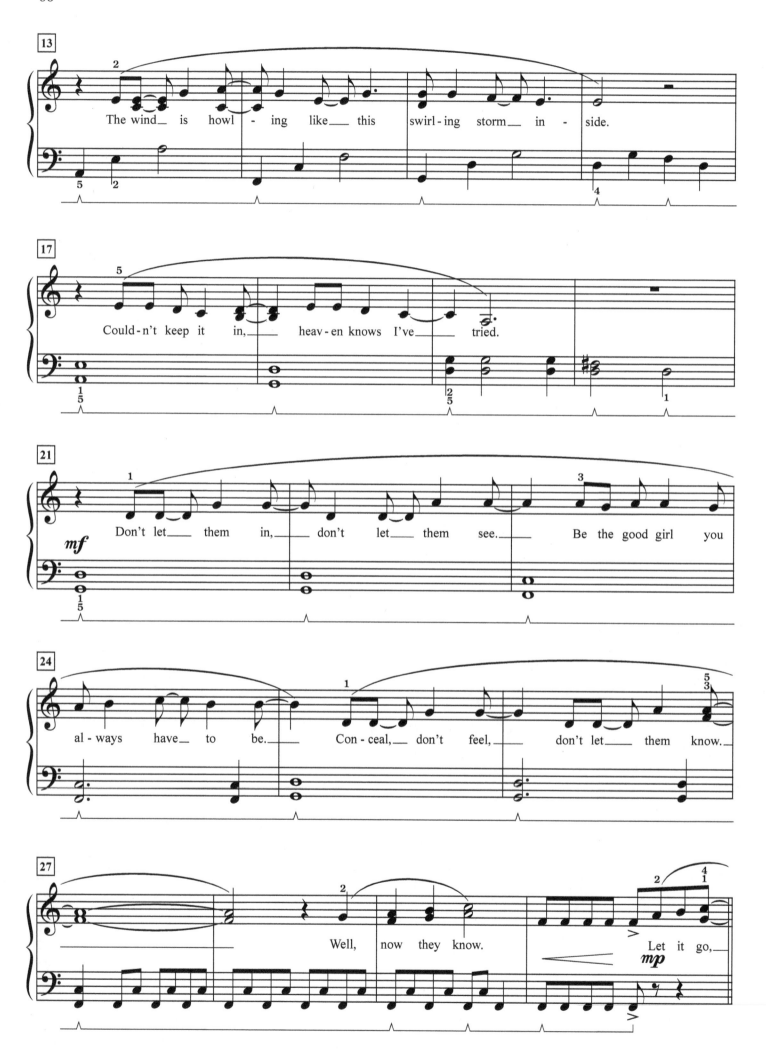

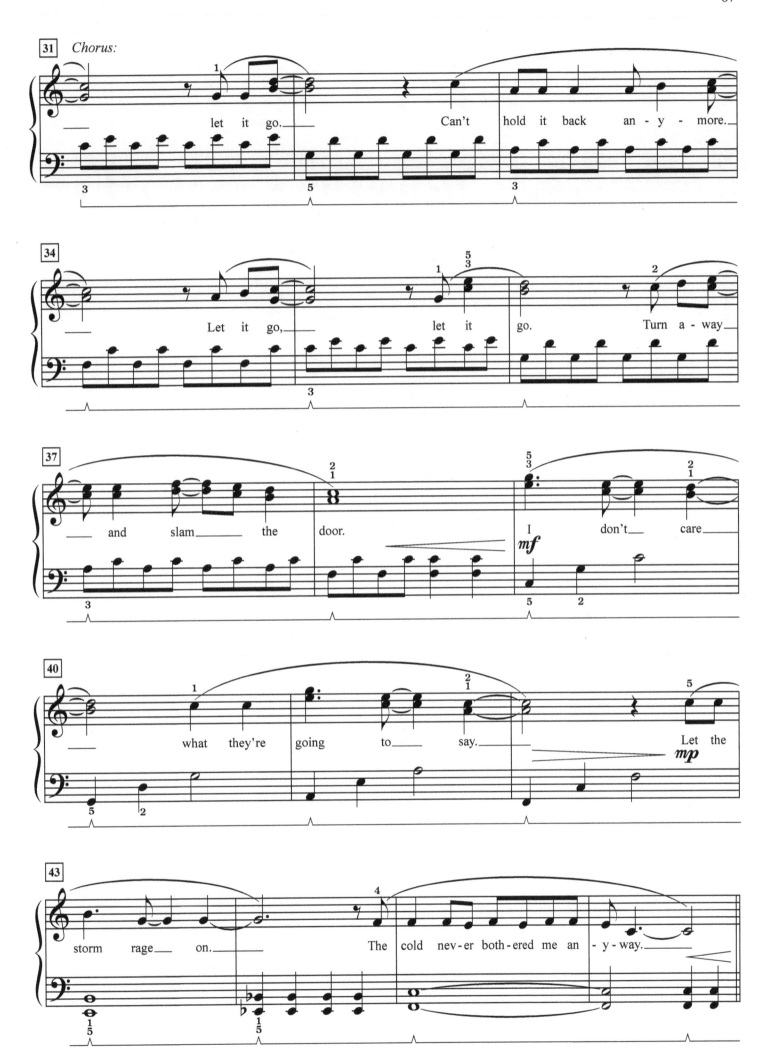

Misty

Words by Johnny Burke
Music by Erroll Garner
Arr. Dan Coates

Slowly, with expression

My Funny Valentine

Words by Lorenz Hart
Music by Richard Rodgers
Arr. Dan Coates

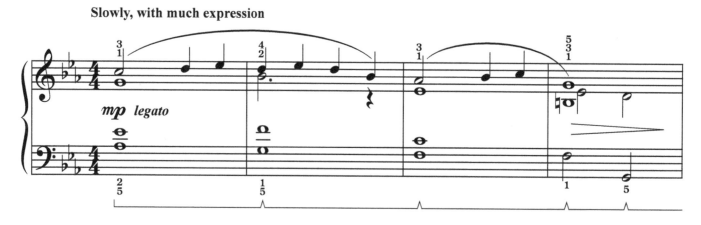

Your looks are laugh - a - ble, un - pho - to - graph - a - ble,

yet you're my fav - 'rite work of art._____ Is your

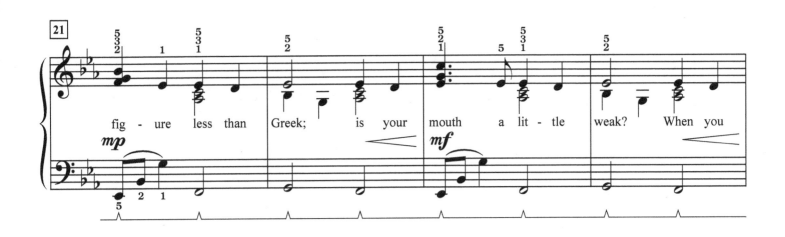

fig - ure less than Greek; is your mouth a lit - tle weak? When you

o - pen it to speak,____ are you smart? But

don't change a hair for me, not if you care for me.

Stay, lit - tle Val - en - tine, stay!

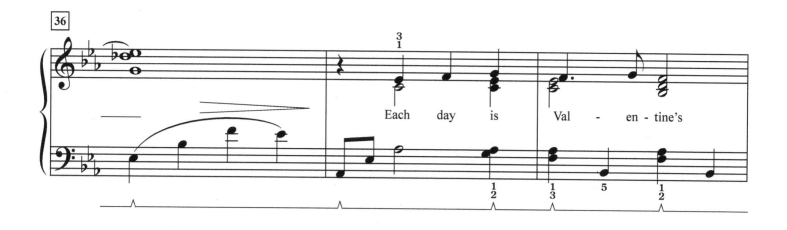

Each day is Val - en - tine's

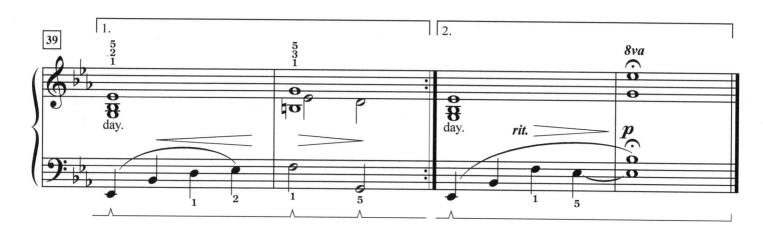

day.

The Notebook

Written by Aaron Zigman
Arr. Dan Coates

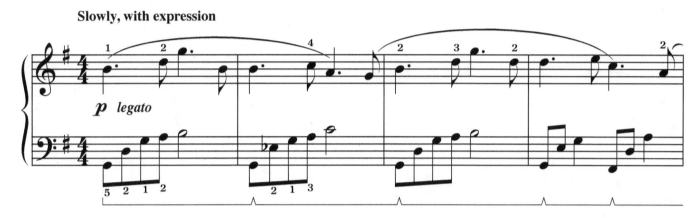

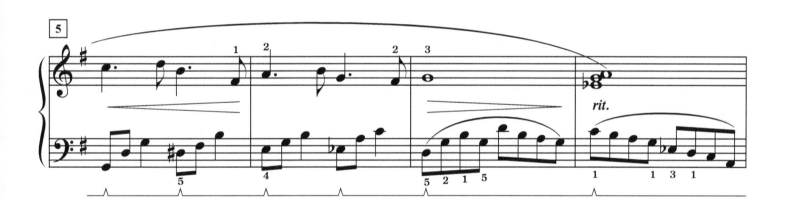

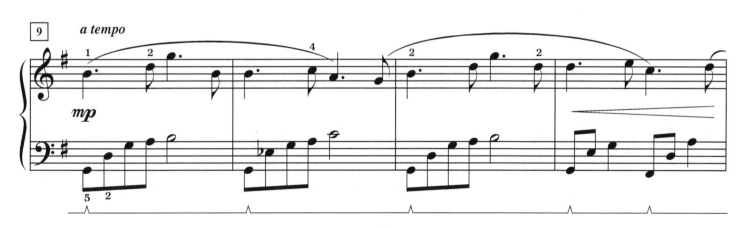

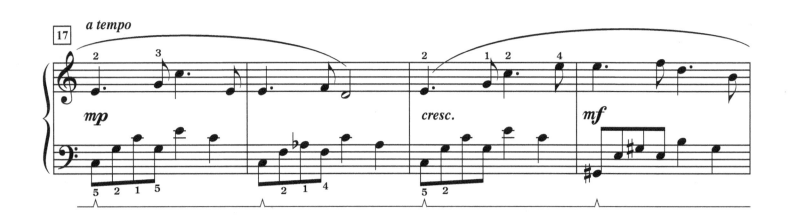

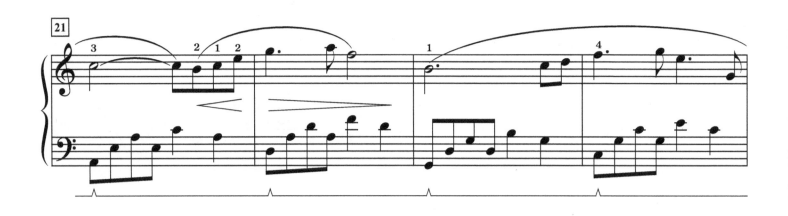

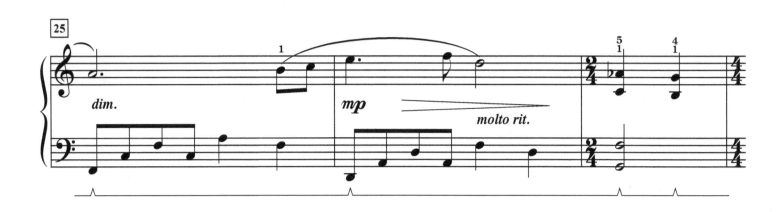

Open Arms

Words and Music by
Jonathan Cain and Steve Perry
Arr. Dan Coates

35 here_____ I am with o - pen arms,___

39 hop - ing to see what your love means to me; o - pen

43 arms.___

47

51

Over the Rainbow

(from *The Wizard of Oz*)

Music by Harold Arlen
Lyrics by E.Y. Harburg
Arr. Dan Coates

Some - where o - ver the rain - bow blue - birds fly.

Birds fly o - ver the rain - bow, why then, oh why can't

I? I?

If hap - py lit - tle blue - birds fly be -

yond the rain - bow, why oh why can't I?

The Pink Panther

By Henry Mancini
Arr. Dan Coates

* Imitate the sound of double bass pizzicatos.

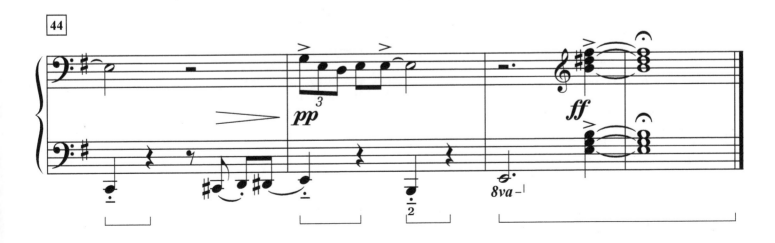

The Prayer

Words and Music by
Carole Bayer Sager and David Foster
Arr. Dan Coates

Slowly, with expression

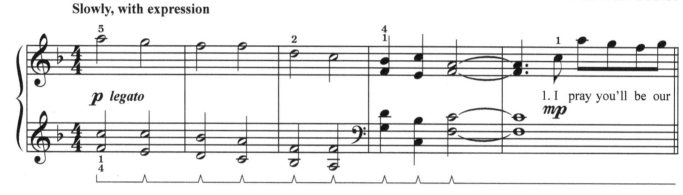

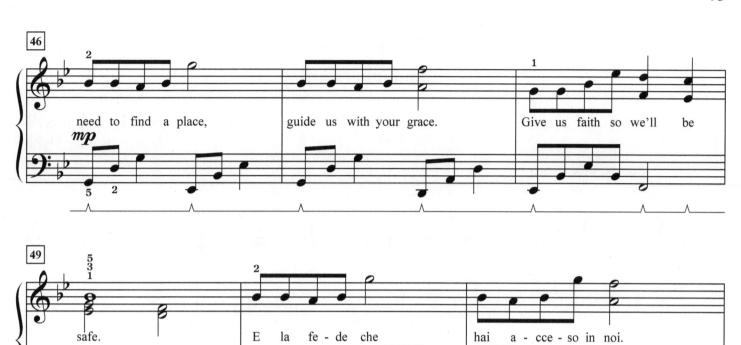

Verse 2 (English lyric):
I pray we'll find your light,
And hold it in our hearts
When stars go out each night.
Let this be our prayer,
When shadows fill our day.
Lead us to a place,
Guide us with your grace.
Give us faith so we'll be safe.

Verse 3 (Italian lyric):
La forza che ci dai
é il desiderio che.
Ognuno trovi amore
Intorno e dentro sé.

People

(from *Funny Girl*)

Words by Bob Merrill
Music by Jule Styne
Arr. Dan Coates

let - ting our grown up pride / hide all the need in - side, act - ing

more / like chil - dren, / than chil - dren.

Lov - ers_____ / are ver - y spe - cial peo - ple,_____ / they're the

luck - i - est peo - ple_____ in the world. / With one

Singin' in the Rain

(from *Singin' in the Rain*)

Music by Nacio Herb Brown
Lyric by Arthur Freed
Arr. Dan Coates

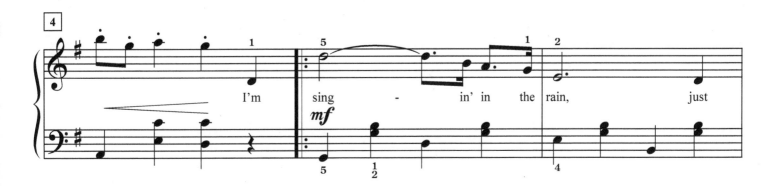

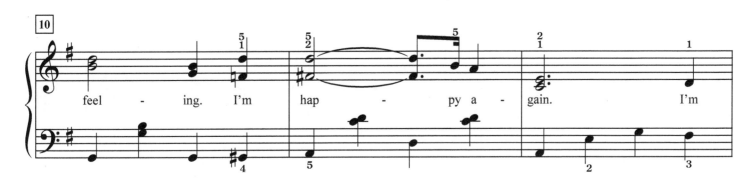

Someone to Watch Over Me

Music and Lyrics by
George Gershwin and Ira Gershwin
Arr. Dan Coates

Star Wars
(Main Theme)

Music by **JOHN WILLIAMS**
Arr. Dan Coates

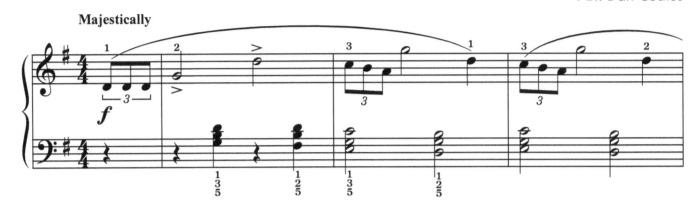

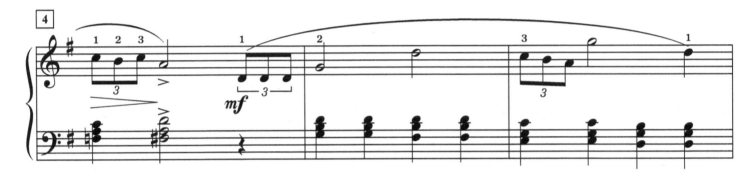

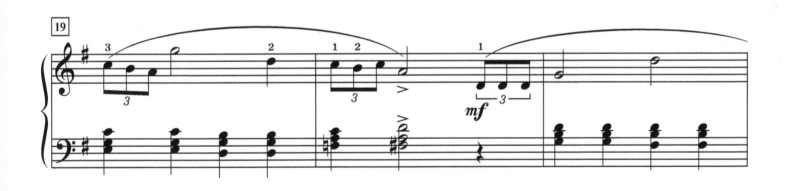

Stairway to Heaven

Words and Music by
Jimmy Page and Robert Plant
Arr. Dan Coates

They Can't Take That Away from Me

Music and Lyrics by
George Gershwin and Ira Gershwin
Arr. Dan Coates

Tomorrow

(from *Annie*)

Music by Charles Strouse
Lyric by Martin Charnin
Arr. Dan Coates

The sun-'ll come out_____ to-mor-row,

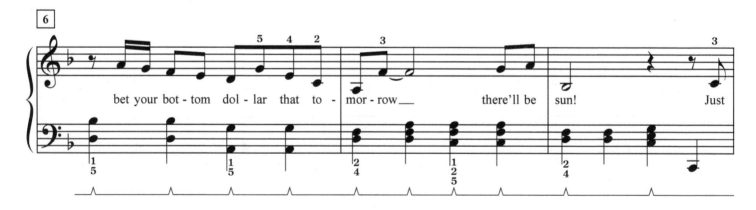

bet your bot-tom dol-lar that to-mor-row___ there'll be sun! Just

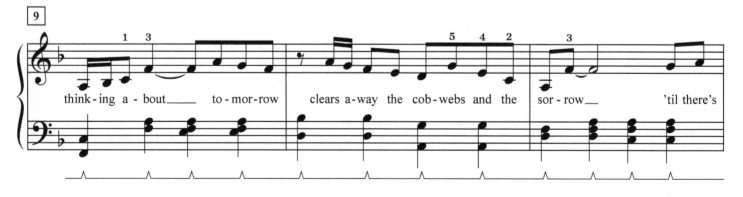

think-ing a-bout___ to-mor-row clears a-way the cob-webs and the sor-row___ 'til there's

mor - row, to - mor - row, I love ya to - mor - row, you're

al - ways a day a - way! To - mor - row, to - mor - row, I

love ya to - mor - row, you're on - ly a day a -

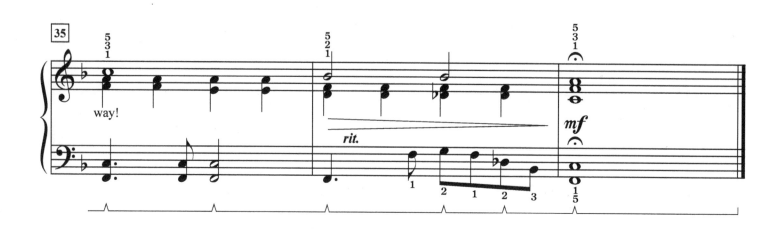

way!

Try to Remember

(from *The Fantasticks*)

Lyrics by Tom Jones
Music by Harvey Schmidt
Arr. Dan Coates

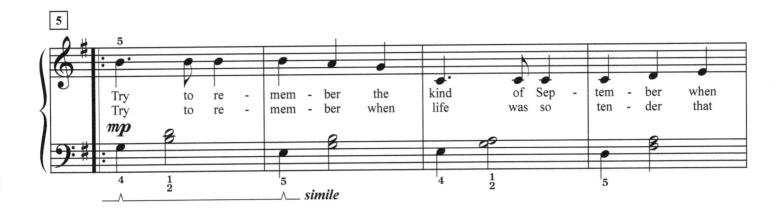

Try to re - mem - ber the kind of Sep - tem - ber when
Try to re - mem - ber when life was so ten - der that

life was slow and oh, so mel - low.
no one wept ex - cept so the wil - low.

116

Try   to re - mem - ber   the   kind   of Sep - tem - ber   when
Try   to re - mem - ber   when   life   was so   ten - der   that

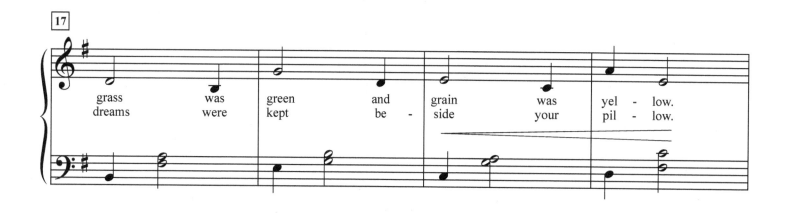

grass   was   green   and   grain   was   yel - low.
dreams   were   kept   be - side   your   pil - low.

Try   to re - mem - ber   the   kind   of Sep - tem - ber   when
Try   to re - mem - ber   when   life   was so   ten - der   that

you   were   a   ten - der   and   cal -   low   fel - low.
love   was   an   em - ber   a - bout   to   bil - low.

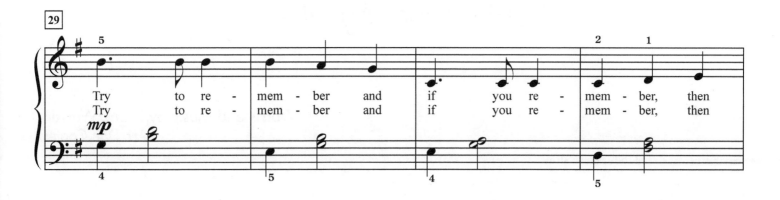

Try   to re - mem - ber   and   if   you re - mem - ber,   then
Try   to re - mem - ber   and   if   you re - mem - ber,   then

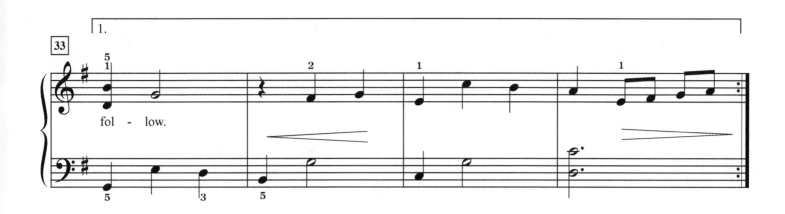

1.

fol - low.

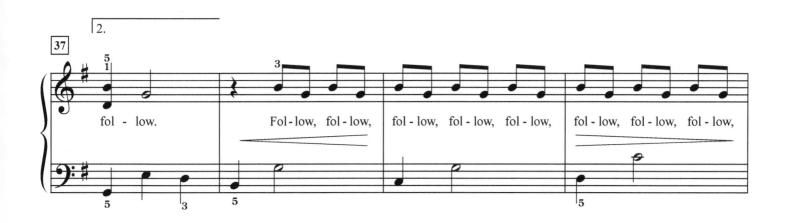

2.

fol - low.   Fol-low, fol-low,   fol-low, fol-low, fol-low,   fol-low, fol-low, fol-low,

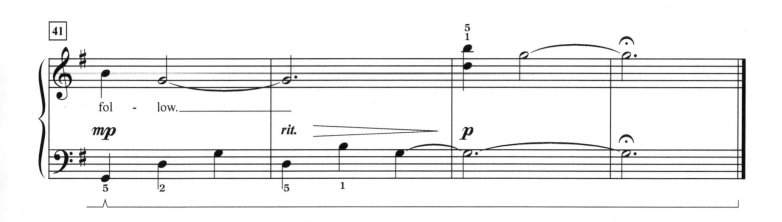

fol - low.

Un-break My Heart

Words and Music by Diane Warren
Arr. Dan Coates

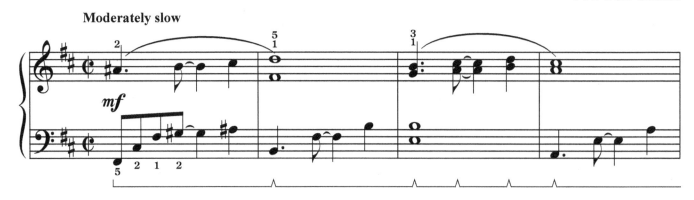

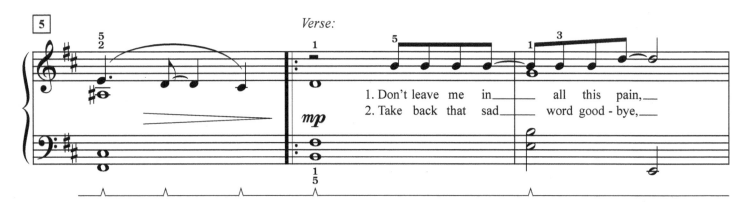

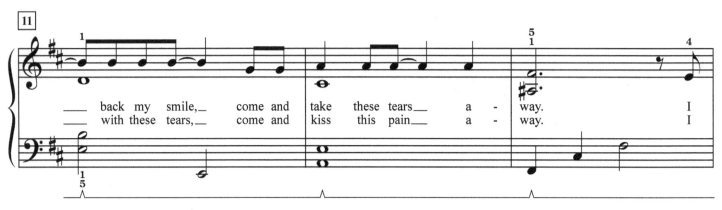

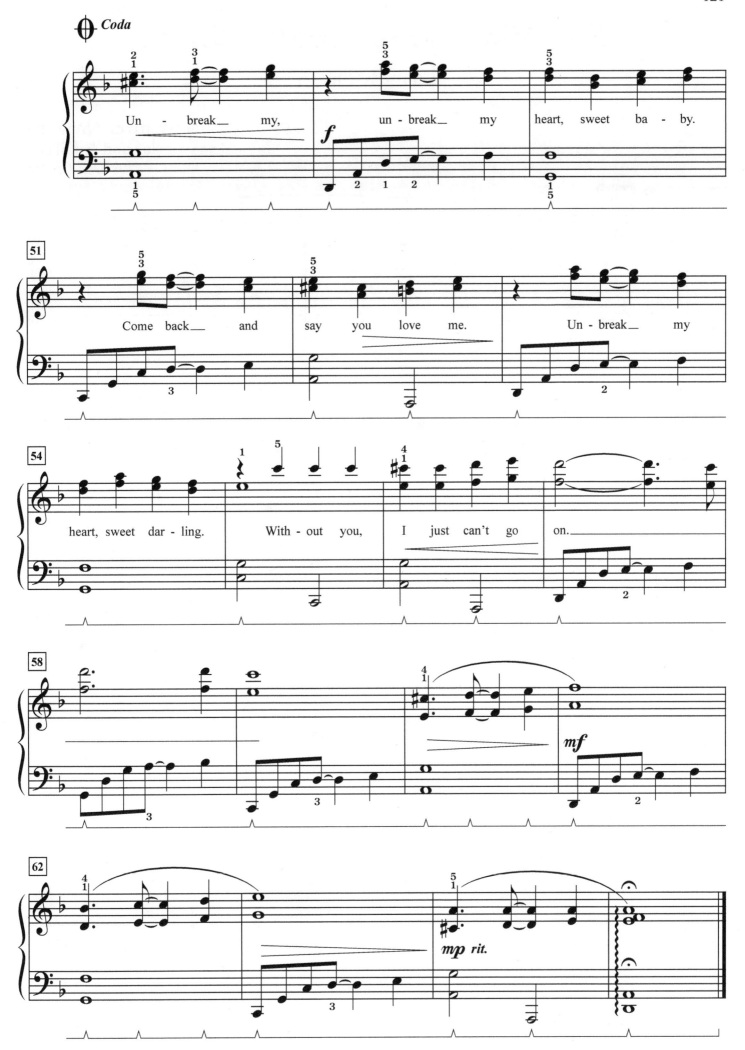

The Wind Beneath My Wings

(from *Beaches*)

Words and Music by
Larry Henley and Jeff Silbar
Arr. Dan Coates

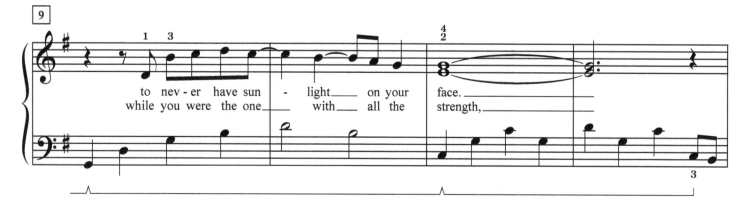

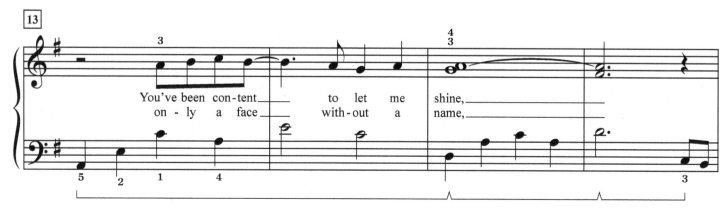

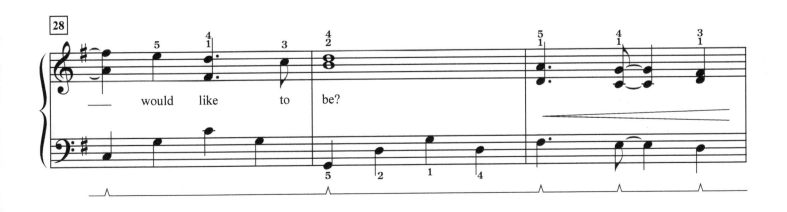

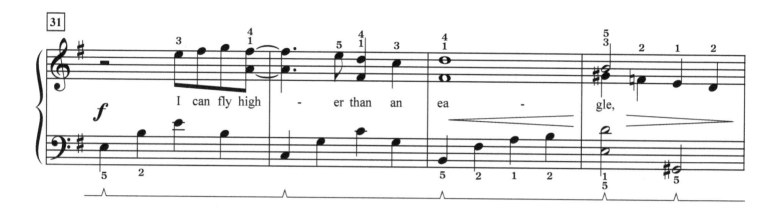

I can fly high - er than an ea - gle,

'cause you are the wind beneath my wings.

You are the wind beneath my wings.

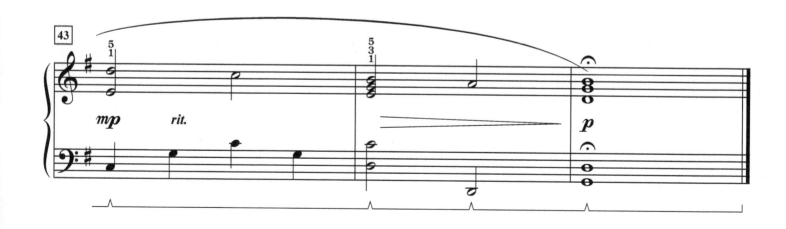

A Whole New World

(from Walt Disney's *Aladdin*)

Words by Tim Rice
Music by Alan Menken
Arr. Dan Coates

Chorus:

world,_____ a new fan - tas - tic point___ of

view. No one to tell us no or where to go or

say we're on - ly dream - ing. A whole new world,_____

—— a daz - zling place I nev - er knew. But when I'm

way up here it's crys-tal clear that now I'm in a whole new world with

you. A whole new world, that's where we'll

be. A thrill-ing chase, a won-d'rous

place, for you and me.

You Raise Me Up

Words and Music by
Rolf Lovland and Brendan Graham
Arr. Dan Coates